Amazing, vivid, and inspiring

Coralie Banks, BA, FCMC

I highly recommend this fascinating and informative read to everyone, believer, and non-believer alike, to discover rich nuggets about Heaven and about God's heart for all mankind. It will greatly encourage you, and change your perspective regarding your future in eternity, and definitely, even toward your life here on earth! It will also confirm or challenge what you already know, or think you know!

Helena Sherlock, Professional

The first thing that struck me when reading Karen's book was remembrance of a Bible passage (2 Corinthians 12:2): "I know a man in Christ who fourteen years ago—whether in the body I do not know, or whether out of the body I do not know, God knows—such a one was caught up to the third heaven."

On completing reading the book, another Bible quote occurred to me (Luke18:16): "Suffer little children to come unto me, and forbid them not, for of such is the kingdom of God. Truly I say to you, whoever does not receive the kingdom of God like a child shall not enter it at all." This, because Karen writes as an eager child, regardless of a possibly skeptical audience. This woman is on a mission.

Karen honestly and boldly writes of her experiences. Thank you for breaking out of the box Karen!

Val Kendall Ph.D., R.Psych.

More from Karen McKenzieSmith:

"WHAT A LIFE! ... THINGS MY CHILDREN DON'T KNOW ABOUT THEIR MOTHER!"

Available on Amazon, or it can be ordered through Chapters or any sister bookstore.

"WHAT AM I GOING TO DO WITH THIS CHILD? 3 EASY STEPS TO SUCCESSFUL PARENTING"

Category bestseller available on-line through Amazon or ordered through the kiosk at any Chapters, or any sister bookstores.

Discounts are available on bulk purchases of this book for reselling, educational resources, gifts, or fundraising.

You can also contact the author to arrange a workshop, talk, or presentation for your local group.

karencowgirl@shaw.ca
https://www.facebook.com/karen.m.smith.9843

Welcome to Heaven

Revealing My Visits

Drawing by the author
Karen McKenzieSmith

Dedication

To all whom are looking for Heaven and God's peace in your life. And to God, thank you for eternal life.

Contents

Introduction

"With man, this is impossible…
All things are possible with God."
Mark 10:27

*What's happening to me!? It is so good! Is it real? I am so
confused. Was this really happening? Shouldn't I have
died, or had I actually died? Am I crazy?*

*I know I've been here more than once. It's been many
times! I sense no timeframe, at least no sense of time like
we have on earth.*

*When I return to earth the time is exactly the same as
when I left.*

It happens to me, just like it has to so many others. As I wrote this book, I read about quite a few other people's Near-Death Experiences (NDE's), and I could see genuine similarities that increased my faith that it was real.

Only my experiences had one big difference: I didn't have to actually physically die in order to get there!How do I know that I actually went to Heaven?

I just knew in my very being that what I was experiencing was Heavenly. Plus, I have seen the same things others have seen. When I read about their experiences as I prepared this book, I was having "Ahhhahhh!" moments all the way through!

I'm so very glad that others have seen what I've seen. Their descriptions of their NDE's are often very similar to mine and it verifies that I'm not crazy or making these things up. It assures me that others know what I know and are sharing their stories too. That they too felt compelled to tell of their experiences.

Now I know it's not an easy thing to believe someone who says they have been to Heaven and back numerous times. Which is why throughout this book I may refer to others' NDE's that align with my experiences. Crazy doesn't enter into the equation at all. Because quite a few others reporting NDE's would have to be crazy too.

Up until now I haven't really told anyone these stories. Yet they have changed me very much. (All in a good way!) I have grown so much more spiritually because of them. I feel blessed and all the wiser to experience Heaven as well as to help when I go there. I love to be able to help!

Sometimes I wish that I could simply stay in Heaven forever. However, I do know that the Lord is not finished with me yet here on earth. Sometimes when I'm on an airplane and notice others that are afraid to fly, I want to reassure them by saying, "Not to

2

worry, if I'm on this flight it won't crash, because God isn't finished with me yet! LOL!" It's my passion to help Him in any way I can right here on earth. I'm honoured to help my Trinity (God, Jesus, and the Holy Spirit) in any way I possibly can!

One thing I do know is, I can't go back to life as it was. To find out more about the many ways I have helped my Trinity over the years, please read my autobiography: "WHAT A LIFE! ...things my children don't know about their Mother!" available on Amazon, (or it can be ordered through Chapters or any sister bookstore).

Being able to help various times in Heaven has taught me a lot! Especially the importance of it being absolutely necessary not to worry. I know that's easier said than done. If you catch yourself worrying, try to stop it as soon as you can. It is not worth it whatsoever. In fact, worry is sin believe it or not!

Having been to Heaven has shown me that the Trinity has everything under control. That may sound far-fetched to you, but the truth is when Jesus died on the cross, He finished everything for us. He achieved the victory! That means the things we go through here on earth are not worth worrying over. And those trials will actually end up being blessings in disguise!

I know that leaving worry behind sounds impossible. Realizing I don't need to worry has made my life much better. By not worrying, I am able to enjoy and relax more trustingly in the Trinity.

I feel compelled now to tell the story of my trips to Heaven. This is mainly because the Lord told me that it was time, and that people need to start knowing that there is a Heaven and a hell, and they need to know how to get to Heaven!

Also thinking about the afterlife emphasizes our need to make use of our time on earth in the best way possible. For me, the best use of my time is to tell this story to you!

God works through us all the time, every single day. That may sound bizarre, but it surely isn't to me!

So here I am, about to try and describe the indescribable. It's something so incredible that there aren't even words in the English vocabulary to express it all! Please forgive and accept my limited attempts. Hopefully, they will inspire you to hope for something brighter, bigger, and more amazing than you have ever seen on earth!

It was suggested to me by my editor to write this book in an illustrated form. Yet that too presents a problem. For nothing in the form of colours that we have on earth can depict accurately the colours I connected with in Heaven. Yes, I connected with the colours. It seemed to me that the colours and/or the objects were alive and glad to see me. Hence, I connected with them.

I have added a beautiful illustration from one of my concept drawings to help you visualize and appreciate the revelation I was given relating to the crucifixion.

4

We Can Choose Heaven or Not

"Set your mind on things above,
not on earthly things."
Colossians 3:2

Knowing what happens after death relieves you of concerns around the inevitable. One's death, and death of our loved ones will happen. And then what?

One thing is for sure; Heaven is real and I'm not dreaming this stuff up!

How could there not be a Heaven? Why wouldn't there be one? What would be so bad about there being a Heaven anyway? You don't have to go there yourself to know it exists when way too many others' NDE's, assure you that it is there.

Another piece of good news I've discovered regarding all these trips to Heaven is I definitely know there's a place that I'm going to after I die!

God leaves it up to your free will to choose Heaven or not. You can choose to have Him in your life to help and protect you, or not. "We are either in the process of resisting God's truth or in the process of being shaped and modelled by his truths." Charles Stanley [1]

**Do you know
where you are going
when you die?**

[1] pg.35 'To Heaven And Back' by Mary C. Neil, MD.

Hell Vs. Heaven

God does not want to see anyone suffer! He doesn't want hell and evil to exist, but he gave us "free will". So, when a third of the angels in Heaven chose to not follow God but rather satan instead, God gave them their own kingdom, hell, to rule.

Take Hitler for example. It's my opinion that Hitler could possibly be in Heaven! Now I know that sounds shocking and appalling. However, let's just stop and think for a second. Hitler could've chosen at the very last minute of his life to follow God and Jesus. On his deathbed, Hitler could've gone one way or the other. He could've chosen to follow God and Jesus, therefore entering Heaven! Or he could have denied them and turned away completely, therefore being given hell to live in.

God won't force anyone to follow Him. It boils down to our own freedom to choose which way we're going to go. Are we going to follow His will? Or follow our own? Are we going to follow God and inherit Heaven? Or are we going to deny Him and inherit hell? When we go by our own nature/flesh, or our own will then we don't inherit Heaven. We are cast out of Heaven.

Time is given on earth to go through examples of good and evil, allowing us the opportunity of free will to choose either/or. I suppose you could say that's the reason both suffering and evil exist along with good. Suffering and pain, good and evil exist on earth to give us each many options and opportunities to choose Him!

If we don't choose Him, and some don't, then we're cast out of Heaven and where is the option to go if you're cast out of Heaven? It is hell! Where a third of the angels have fallen from Heaven to rule under satan, the devil. Although I have never been to hell, there have been some NDE'ers that report they have.

I Have Seen God

> "Moreover, no man knows
> when his hour will come."
> Ecclesiastes 9:12

I see my name as prophetic. "KAREN" means Pure of Heart. There is a verse in the Bible that states…" the pure of heart shall see God" (Matthew 5:8), and I see God!

There is another verse in the Bible that says… "those that see God shall die!" (Deuteronomy 18:16).

Since I started writing this book and telling people about it, some fellow Christians have responded negatively to my telling them about actually having seen God! Knowing how they would react is another reason why I have kept this #1 experience of mine to myself for years!

I agree, one does die when they see GOD! However, my body does not physically die! I die to my "flesh". Which is exactly what happened to me when I did come face to face with God!

The minute I set foot in His Throne Room for the very first time, I fell prostrate on the floor! There was no doubt in my mind this was Heaven, and I was truly in the presence of God! He says the peace He gives is a peace the world cannot give (John 14:2). And He freely gives it, free of charge, without any cost to you or me. This incredible peace and endearing, soft- spoken approach toward me means something very dear to me. It proves that He truly is non-judgmental. As a result, there was no question. I felt completely safe. This has increased my faith.

Every time I'm in Heaven I feel so much love, filling me up to overflowing, coming from everyone and everything. And I mean everything! People, plants, animals, even colour! It comes from every direction. A deeply heartfelt greeting of acceptance. A kind of warm and welcoming feeling that we don't experience on earth unless maybe you are a queen in a parade and the star attraction!

Although that description I just gave might actually diminish the warmth I feel in Heaven. I feel so special! I have never felt such a deep sense of belonging as I do there. I feel respected and more appreciated than ever, and all without proving a thing! I do not need, nor does anyone need to prove anything in Heaven. I'm just plain accepted as I am, warts and all. LOL! I actually don't think in Heaven we will have warts but if we did, I don't think they'll be noticed by anyone, nor be a health issue.

All through my life, right from childhood, I've never been one to live inside the box, so to speak. Therefore, I'm not likely to be met with lots of camaraderie or mutual agreement from others. Having been a pioneer of many things throughout my life definitely puts me on the outside sometimes, regardless of my desire to fit in. Or rather just simply to be accepted, whether one agrees or disagrees with me.

Einstein said something once that makes perfect sense to me and explains my life to a "Tee": "Those with creativity will *always* be met with *violent* opposition from mediocrity!" (If you wish to read further on this particular aspect of my life, check out my autobiography "WHAT A LIFE...things my children don't know about their Mother!" There is a chapter on "Persecution"

At any rate, the more I got to know my Father God, my Daddy, the more I realized how true He was to His word. Scripture says in Psalm 15:2 that He speaks and holds truth in His heart. The Bible says He does not judge, and He really doesn't! He is so accepting of the way I am. Not expecting me to be anything more. He loves me just the way I am.

Which makes sense. After all He's the one that created us, and He doesn't make junk! It says right in the bible, we were created in His own image (Gen: 1:27).

"I praise you because I am fearfully and wonderfully made; your works are wonderful; I know that full well." (Psalm 139:14)

Other NDE'ers frequently expressed their admiration at how His great presence affected them. Gary sums it up as being: "...filled with awe at His beautiful presences." [2]

His work is awesome! (Psalm 66:5)

[2] pg 278 Imagine Heaven, by John Burke.

Hermitage

I've occasionally felt compelled to press in spiritually towards God more closely than usual. On those occasions, I've gone on a "hermitage". These would typically last several days. While on a hermitage, I would spend virtually the entire time in prayer talking to my Trinity. This includes talking to them face to face.

I can't recall exactly when it was, I was going through a time period when I was pleading with God and Jesus to reveal Heaven ON earth to me. You see, often when saying the Lord's prayer, I would ponder over this with Jesus. I would ask to not have to go to Heaven but to see it here on earth as it was stated in the Lord's prayer (i.e., "thy kingdom come, thy will be done on earth as it is in Heaven"). Hence, He did exactly that for me! I began to see glimpses of Heaven right here on earth!

As you continue to read, there are stories throughout this book that give examples of this. Off the top of my head I would have to say, first and foremost, a magnificent glimpse of Heaven on earth, is creation itself! All that God created around us, on this magnificent, glorious planet called home.

Nature and all the animals and creatures large and small. Everything just shouts Heaven on earth!

Anyhow, at some point during my hermitage and my relentless pressing-in, it happened. I was sitting on a bench overlooking a deep ravine in the foothills outside Calgary at King's Fold retreat. My pressing-in had paid off on this particular hermitage. Jesus stood beside me as we talked.

After we had conversed a while, Jesus paused. Then Jesus simply said to me, "Come with me; I have something to show you."

He took me by the hand and the next thing I knew I was outside the entry door to the Throne Room. That was the most beautiful, awe-inspiring door I had ever set eyes on. Who would have thought? For I never even asked to go to Heaven.

Upon setting foot in the door, I dropped to the floor, but it wasn't out of fear. It was out of loyalty, humility, and gratitude. A definite admiration filled with a deep respect.

During their peek into Heaven, many NDE'ers report the very things scripture tells us about Heaven and the afterlife, especially in the book of Revelation, the last book in the Bible.

Many NDE'ers confirm, as I do too, the personal loving all-knowing nature of this Being I refer to and believe to be God. So unconditional with His love! Non-condemning and sincerely caring and empathetic toward anyone and everyone.

My #1 Experience

"He is the light of the world...
Who came to reveal the unseen."
John 14:1

It seems to me that Heaven is not something God wants to keep hidden from us. In fact, more the opposite. God definitely wants us to know Heaven can be easily accessed.

Heaven is even accessible before we die! Either right here on earth or by trips to Heaven!

What makes me think this? It comes from what God said to me on my first trip to His Throne Room. How we got there I'll never know. All I know is we got there in a nanosecond from earth to outside those massive doors, in not even a blink of an eye.

During that specific hermitage was the very first time I literally went to Heaven. Jesus took me right up to an incredibly huge and magnificent door of glistening solid gold! It seemed to glow! This door was so tall that it rose up out of sight.

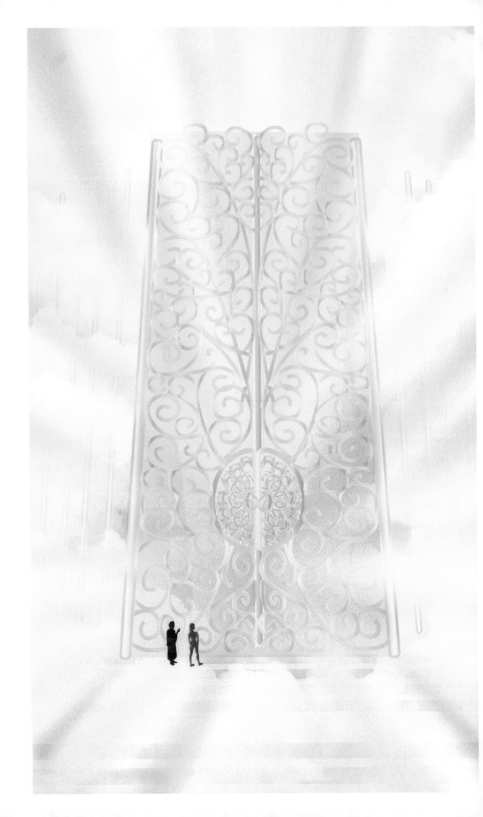

I couldn't see the top of it in the mist overhead. It was like we were in a cloud and the only visible thing was this gigantic door. I loved the doorknob, it was embossed gold, round and huge, smack in the centre of the massive golden door! Just by looking at it, Jesus opened it!

However, it was not the brightness that caused me to fall to the floor. It was the holiness! I just had to fall to the floor prostrate. Not even lifting my head a centimeter off the floor. I was in such reverence of my holy dear God that I could not do anything else but remain in that state. There have been a few times in my life where I've felt extreme holiness and humility come over me. Holiness that just went right through my body and filled me right up! I felt a definite admiration filled with a deep respect. In this way I could truly worship Him! There was no doubt in my mind, this was Heaven and I was in God's presence!

This time I would have to say was one of those where I felt the most holy, I have ever felt in my entire life!

My body and my very being wouldn't allow me to go any further. It wasn't Jesus holding me back from going any further. I simply could not budge myself. I was "too moved to move", as funny and as ironic that may sound. That was it exactly. It was such a HOLY atmosphere, I could do nothing more than fall on my face, before Him, my God.

That's what moved me to not move while on my face. Given that, I knew I must be in the presence of God! It was confirmed by His voice! For He spoke very clearly and very regally. He literally spoke out loud. It was not telepathy by which He spoke.

There was this incredible peace and calm that emanated from Him and from His voice. Along with it was a love beyond measure. Words like stateliness, grandness, impressiveness, or magnificence and majesty don't even come close to describing the royal kingly state of this all-sufficient One I call God!

I'm not sure how much time actually lapsed. But I do remember very clearly what God said to me when we went to leave.

He said, "You will come back, won't you?"

I said in a very shaky stuttering, but reverent way, "Y-you mean I can?"

God said, "Why wouldn't I want my children to visit me?"

Just as we were about to turn and leave, God said one more thing that was so precious and yet a bit on the funny side. God is funny! He said, "And when you come back for a visit, I promise I will dim the light a bit for you."

As I left with Jesus escorting me back to earth, I felt like crying over all those years I never visited Him.

It made me think of a time when I was in Explorers at the church around the age of 12 or 13. We were each assigned to visit an elderly person in one of the nursing homes near where I lived. I was always saddened by the number of patients there who seemed to have no one ever come visit them.

So, when God said that to me, that's the vision that came to mind. Seeing all those individual elderly people sitting alone in each of their rooms.

Sadly, I didn't go back right away to visit God again. It took me a little while to build up enough courage to go again, though I'm not really sure why. Now that I've been back several times I don't hesitate whatsoever to go back to talk to Him about things that are hurting me or to go back to Him and dance with Him over the fun times we've had together.

Sometimes, believe it or not, we even dance like a father and daughter at a wedding. Or hippy-hop around like a father and daughter would dance to Ring-Around-the-Rosie! Sometimes I run to Daddy to fix my hurts, my "boo boos". Other times I just simply sit on His lap while he holds me, and we talk or I sleep in His arms.

Interestingly enough, when I am with God in the Throne Room, I revert back to being a child. I am this eight-year-old innocent child, void of fleshly, worldly thinking. Yet when I am with Jesus, I am myself at the age that I am now.

I can't say for sure why this happens. Although I would have to think that it has to do with God only seeing me in my innocent self, at around age eight. Where Jesus of course sees me as I am now in my sin nature and all.

God is a perfect Daddy to me! An ideal dad! After all, God is perfect in every way!

I hope you'll consider this to be a message to you if you may be afraid of God because you've had an experience that caused you to be afraid of a father figure. I hope this reassures you and lets you know that God would never be one for you to be afraid of. I hope you'll trust in this enough to explore that with Him, Father God, Abba Father.

By the way, yes, He did dim the light after the first time I was there. The light actually comes from Him. That's what lights all of Heaven and energizes it in every imaginable way you could ever think of. That's why I couldn't see anything that first time in the Throne Room. I saw nothing but blinding light.

What Does Jesus Look Like?

A few times people have asked me what Jesus looks like. I have resisted telling them, because I believe He appears to each of us in the way we would receive Him best. That means the way I see Him may be entirely different to the way someone else sees Him. For example, when I lived in Africa, I noticed many Christian families had the "Last Supper", framed and hanging on their wall. In these pictures, all of the disciples and Jesus were black!

I have no problem sharing here what my Jesus looks like to me. I just want to make it clear, that may not be the way Jesus will appear to you. So please do not expect to have Him look exactly like the Jesus I describe.

The way I see Him, He doesn't have dark hair nor is it as long as most pictures depict. My Jesus has shoulder length hair, or even a bit shorter actually. Plus, it's more of a light brown to almost blonde in colour, not dark brown and definitely not black.

When He has been with me, He's almost always wearing a gown or a tunic-like pure white garment. The white is brighter than any white I've ever seen, and it seems energized and stimulating!

Only a few times has He been dressed in what I would call the contemporary dress of today. Once He actually wore black denim jeans, and a dress shirt with shoes and socks, not sandals.

Angels Here, There, Everywhere

"Are not all angels ministering spirits sent to accomplish God's
will and serve those who will inherit salvation?"
Hebrews 1:14

Angels With Us

Often angels are with me, either here on earth or in Heaven. A few
of my trips have consisted of being shown around Heaven by
individual angels or people.

I recall one of those times. It was a very sad time in my life. I was
so extremely depressed at the time. That's when the angels rallied
around me and did their very, very best to cheer me up and keep
me happy in spite of the extremely low time I was going through.

Most of the time the angels spend their time helping me warfare
against demonic forces surrounding me wherever I travel in the
world.

One particular time comes to mind. I was complaining to the Lord about the struggle I was having warding off the enemy. I pleaded with the Lord to take away or at least decrease some of the struggles I was having.

That's when the Lord showed me what was ahead of me, and what the angels were doing.

He showed me hundreds of angels clearing my path, proceeding just ahead of me. They were fighting great battles of warfare. Battles against the demonic presence that was trying to keep me from doing any ministry whatsoever wherever I happen to be in the world.

Angels On Earth

I've seen the archangel Michael on earth at different times and Gabriel at other times.

Michael came to my condo at a time when I was crying out to the Lord for protection from evil that had been ferociously bombarding me. He stood there outside my condo in his robe and sandals, more than three stories high, with the biggest sword I had ever seen! The sword was, like 19 feet tall, (579 centimeters, almost 6 meters). He stood on guard for the longest time, until he wasn't needed anymore. Thank you, Michael!

Shortly after my divorce, thousands of angels of different sizes, surrounded me to help me get through the hell I was going through. I remember specifically a time where they were desperately trying to make me happy.

I was so sad during the divorce, that it literally was impossible for them to make me happy.

Of course, there's always the four angels that sit on the roof of my car and watch over me from every direction as I drive. Especially during the time when a death wish was still on me. That literally meant I was on a hit list for almost 50 years. I was getting, among other things, nearly hit by other vehicles over that time period. Thanks to my four angels, it was to no avail!

Angels Watch Over Us

One thing I love to hear and see when I'm in Heaven is what the angels do as they watch us on earth. When they observe us down on earth, they stop everything and break out in praise when someone does something for God and the Lord. Or when a person asks Jesus into their life.

Angels, and all of Heaven, shared their feelings of joy with me when love was expressed, and they shared their disappointment and sadness when we hurt one another down on earth.

Jesus Christ and all the angels show their delight with major celebrations when we do certain things. They also show their disappointment and sadness for the other things we all do that aren't so good by going into serious prayer and warfare on our behalf. Rest assured. You may think no one has ever prayed for you. That's very wrong. Somebody up there and I mean more than one, is praying for you at all times! Just so you know.

They sing everywhere and at any given time they will break out in celestial song. They get especially excited and sing with such ecstasy whenever anyone on earth comes to the Lord. (Coming to the Lord means simply asking Jesus to become their Lord and Saviour and asking Him to forgive them for their sins!)

It is so reassuring to know that we are being watched over and covered in prayer. All of mankind is God's main concern. He loves us so much that He gave His one and only Son to come to earth. Then in a few short years, (33 of them), His son Jesus Christ died for us, so we can be, if we choose, saved from our sins and death. In other words, "you're to die for"!

That really excites me too, Amen! That he would actually die for me and you! That I have a ticket to Heaven through Jesus Christ, my Saviour! Such magnificent, grandiose love is spread everywhere, and the source is God!

All we have to do in order to obtain freedom from death and sin, is simply to ask Jesus to forgive us our sins and become our Lord and Saviour. Otherwise, sadly, satan has dibs on you if you don't accept Jesus Christ as your Lord and Saviour.

It is only through Jesus that we can achieve eternal life in Heaven. (1 John 4:15, Rev. 2:7) "Seek and you will find; knock and the door will be opened to you." (Matthew 7:7) This allows us to get our name into the "Lamb's Book of Life." (Rev. 3:5, Rev. 13:8 & .20:15) For Salvation is found in no one else but Jesus Christ!

You may think when you read Revelation, that it's something too outrageous to be real, an allegory of sorts. However, I believe it is the most prophetic book in the entire Bible.

Jesus says that He is the way the truth and the life; no one comes to the Father but through Him. (John 14:6).

Angels I Have Heard On High

Heaven is full of celestial song!

During my numerous visits, I couldn't help but hear the angels singing. Praise is continual in Heaven. Angels are everywhere in song, like the ones whistling or humming while they work. And when people and angels worship, it goes directly to Father God in the Throne Room and He reverberates it back. Everything thrives and is electrified in this manner!

Worship applied on earth fulfills so many needs that we don't even realize. Worship has a place; far more important than quite a few Christians may think. It is a role far greater than simply singing a few songs in church as fillers before the sermon.

Worship is medicine to our soul. Therefore, it's extremely important here on earth, just as it is in Heaven. It's God's way of ministering to each of us personally. It is one of His many ways of communicating with us and teaching us. It's a way of healing and mending our woundedness.

It's a great way for him to refuel us, re-energize us and provide much of what we need on so many levels. Worship is like oxygen in Heaven! It is one way our Father God can connect with us.

That's why in the Bible Jesus said, "Lean not on your own understanding but in all your ways acknowledge Him and He shall direct your path!" (Proverbs 3:5-6)

I've heard songs of praise being sung almost non-stop virtually everywhere in Heaven. Celestial songs like I've never heard before and unmatched by any choir anywhere on earth!

One time behind God's throne there was a choir of angels so massive I couldn't count them all. They rose through the roof and their singing rose too, like nothing I've ever heard on this planet of ours. Not from any bird or instrument or any vocal cords.

To tell you the truth, I have never seen the roof. If it is there, it is so high up that I only see the choir of angels disappearing into the mist.

A massive group of singing angels seem to frequent the Throne Room. They remain in the background rising up and beyond in glorious songs of praise.

They are unbelievably magnificent! It may sound silly but the word "angelic "comes to mind as the only word I can find that comes close to describing their sounds. Grand songs of celebration and praises that they continually sing.

Have you ever been to a performance where the singing was so incredibly magnificent that it gave you goose bumps? That it moved your very soul? When you were almost breathless from all the incredible vocal sounds you were hearing? Well that's as close as I can come to describing the sound of the angels singing in Heaven.

Duty Calls

When in the Throne Room with my Daddy, Father God, I'm usually focused on only the two of us. From time to time though, there have been occasions where I've seen various activities going on. Several different times I saw this same activity occur over and over again, only slightly different each consecutive time.

About three or more different times when I was there, I would see the angels all lined up and going through one door and up to Jesus' office desk, then out another door past the desk. They were methodically filing up to His desk, calmly being given individual orders or missions to carry out.

I saw how each time the lineup was longer and got going faster and then faster again, with what seemed like more urgency and concern. I didn't just notice, I sensed it as well! There was such grave urgency in their businesslike actions.

I just love to tell you that Jesus and the angels both don't ever seem the least bit worried or anxious. They are very professional, promptly carrying out the duties necessary to keep as much order as possible, given that we humans on earth have free will!

His office is most elegant, yet efficient. The desk is huge, made of cherrywood and covered with engraving and carvings all over and around it. It is so beautiful! "...for He will command his angels in regard to you, to protect and defend and guard you in all your ways, they will lift you up in their hands..." (Psalm 91:11-12).

I would affirm that for sure! For the Lord has shown me a few different times in my journey the battle going on between the Angels and evil. This was in order to clear the path ahead of me so that I could proceed safely.

I also can confirm angels guard us due to the things I see when I travel to Heaven. Like the duties given out in the Throne Room. Those kinds of things are going on constantly, 24/7, day in and day out! Jesus is always giving out orders to the angels in a calm and orderly manner.

Increased Servanthood

The first time I saw thousands of angels lined up, they were in no hurry. They were just doing their job peacefully and methodically without hesitation, without worry, without any concern whatsoever. The line of angels had no end that I could see.

At different times in the Throne Room, I've seen other things happen. In particular, one thing changed over time. It grew more serious and faster paced as the angels were given their orders. Each consecutive time I visited, they became very busy, very deliberate, and very urgent!

Yet again, amazingly they all still remaining completely calm and unruffled, not seeming worried in the least but very deliberate and speedier about their business.

They simply have a job to do and clearly do it ASAP!

Jesus too seems very calm and very methodical. Not rushed and not strained or worried in the least. Mind you, I have rarely seen Him concerned in any way shape or form and definitely not strained.

As a side note, Jesus does get concerned about us. I know of two main reasons for His concern:

1. He gets concerned when we Christians do not follow through on something, He is prompting us to do, i.e. call someone when we are compelled by Him to do so.

2. Jesus also gets concerned when we Christians don't seem to get connected with Him and act according to the promptings of the Holy Spirit. (Yes, we do "receive the Holy Spirit" when we believe, but not everyone acts on it, and He cares deeply about this.)

My Privileged Duties

I've found another duty occurs occasionally when I've travelled to Heaven. I will meet an individual that will tell me to let their relatives and friends on earth know that they are doing just fine! That they are happy and healthy and at peace. And not to worry a bit about them. Some will also urgently state that they're no longer in pain.

When this happens to me, I get a sense of delight in the duty of having such a message to deliver when I return to earth. I don't set about seeking the person or persons I'm supposed to give the message to. I simply wait and trust wholeheartedly in the Lord to have these people cross my path so that I can deliver the message. This is also another way of affirming that I have the right people to give the message to.

A Waiting Lounge

Many people that have had NDE's write about the guided tour they experienced in Heaven. In the times I took trips to Heaven, I very seldom went on a tour, so to speak. However, one particular time was different.

One of the interesting places I was shown was what appeared to be a waiting lounge. This waiting lounge looked very similar to an elegant and luxurious VIP-owner box in a stadium, such as a hockey or baseball arena.

I'm not sure if it was just for infants, or anyone. The only ones in the room at the time were young ones.

I spotted one in particular. He was off by himself intently watching below, leaning over the window ledge. He seemed to be observing and cheering on something below that I couldn't see. So I asked my guide what he was so attentively watching.

My guide informed me that this little boy was watching his future parents down below on earth!

Just at that moment the boy, overhearing us, turned for half a second to check us out. Uninterrupted, he returned his watchful eyes back to earth.

In that brief glance back at us, I noticed something unusual about the boy. I was seeing a Down Syndrome infant boy monitoring his future parents on earth.

My guide sensed what I was thinking. Immediately I was filled in with some amazing information. I was told that this boy considered it to be an honour to have Down Syndrome! As he sat there excitedly watching from Heaven, this Down Syndrome baby, I was told, was choosing his parents and patiently waiting to be born. Patiently all right, for his parents- to-be were not even married yet!

He actually got to choose to be Down Syndrome, seeing it as an honour. He also saw it as a gift to that couple that were going to be his parents!

I felt that people with Down Syndrome don't see those imperfections as we do or as imperfections at all! They see what we call imperfections as delights, treasures and sought- after achievements. Things to be looked upon as honourable.

I got the impression through the guides (angels), that to have Down Syndrome, was a special thing. The children would actually improve the parents and be teachable opportunities for them. So whatever imperfection a child was born with would turn out to be a blessing in disguise!

Here is a gold nugget, given what I have just shared with you, I hope you will find it encouraging. When it comes to trials in your life, may they become blessings for you!

You may have noticed another curious thing in this last story: my guide sensing what I was thinking. Yes, in Heaven there is no need to actually talk! We easily communicate through thought! That's common throughout the reading I've done on others' NDE's as well. Many others have experienced Heavenly communication in this way, without a word being actually spoken.

I just have to think of a question and my guide angels will answer me. This is an effortless way to gain enormous amounts of special knowledge beyond our understanding on earth.

You may be wondering what my guides looked like. Angels I've come across can look different depending on the task at hand. First of all, some that I've seen have no wings. Yet others have pure white, translucent, enormous wings.

This particular angel in the waiting room was seven feet tall and wore a full-length gown, smock or tunic-like garment. His tunic glowed with the bright white energizing light of God. The angel had the nicest demeanor anyone could have. I felt immediate connection and sincerity.

Now I say, "this angel", because they are not all the same size. I've had some come to save me when I was threatened that are giants! Others are teeny-weenie little cuties!

Some of those experiences were right here on earth! They were not just in Heaven.

Now the story about the little Down Syndrome boy is not over yet! I really don't recall just how much time elapsed between when I saw this boy in Heaven, to when I was in a shopping mall at home in Calgary.

Anyhow, one day back here on earth while in this mall walking towards me, was a man carrying a small child. The boy couldn't have been more than six months old, if that.

Now here's the amazing, somewhat shocking thing that happened. Just as the man got within a few feet of passing by me, the boy turned and looked directly at me! He actually stared right at me, as if knowing full well who I was. Guess what? He had Down Syndrome.

Then just in that moment, he winked at me with an all-knowing smile. Wow! I was hit right away with complete awareness and the recall of that time in Heaven when I spotted him looking down at his parents to be.

Now of course I'll never know for sure if that was the same boy, but for him to turn like that and wink at me, it sure makes me wonder!

Something occurs to me as I recall this story.

If parents are selected, as appears to be the case, then when I see single parents the thought creeps into my mind that we've let these children down when we don't stick together as a couple. What a shame. However, I do realize, and won't argue the fact, there are extenuating experiences that require divorce.

I Met My Dad

On one occasion Jesus came to me and said He had someone that wanted to see me.

Hence another trip to Heaven. Of course, they are always worth it! This one in particular was definitely well worth it for sure! I saw and met my dad!

In my book, "WHAT A LIFE! ...things my children don't know about their Mother!" I share about my relationship with my dad. I looked my whole childhood for his approval. For any kind of recognition from him. In my late teens and early 20s, it finally dawned on me that my dad just wasn't the kind of person that would love in the way a daughter would want them to. I knew then it was important for me to let that go and just appreciate my dad for the way he was.

Given this information I've just shared, you won't believe what happened when I went to Heaven this time. I met my dad!

He actually asked God if he could have a second chance at showing me, his daughter, the kind of love I should've had from him as my dad during his life on earth! Unbelievable!

At the same time as I came into my dad's presence, I became a young child again! He beckoned for me to come and sit on his knee.

As I walked toward him, he reached out and lifted me up on his knee. He gave me the greatest hug I had always dreamed of getting from my dad!

We spent the rest of the time reminiscing and remembering good ole memories. He spent a lot of time telling me how proud he was when I won this award or that competition. Or did this or that.

He even told me he was so proud of me when I saved a little girl and some other kids. I didn't even know he knew anything about that! (Over the years as a lifeguard, I had saved a few children. One in particular had actually drowned but was revived due to my lifesaving efforts. That is the little girl my dad was referring to. Also, in my autobiography, you can read about this.)

This experience had such a profound effect on me that I was able to completely heal my relationship with my dad.

I Saw My Mom Go to Heaven

Initially I saw my mom just after she passed away. She didn't talk to me. Nor did she even look my way.

I saw her walking along a long winding path up towards Heaven. Along the sides of this path were people that were obviously already inhabitants of Heaven. Their white robes were glowing pure light and glistening. As everyone sang or hummed and waved, their tunics swayed to the rhythm. They were waving palm leaves and cheering her on and welcoming her warmly as she proceeded up the beautiful flowery, golden-paved path on her way towards Heaven.

They were just as they are described in the Bible, in the most prophetic book! The book of Revelation. "They were wearing white robes and were holding palm branches in their hands..." (Revelation 7:9).

All were smiling with warm enveloping eyes that revealed kind hearts. Brimming over with unconditional love that flowed out onto my mom!

I didn't recognize anyone. I wasn't really paying attention to them, for my focus was primarily on my mom. Yet I knew they were going to be my Mom's spiritual family and would treat her with the utmost unconditional love that anyone could ever dream of receiving! It was so wonderful to share her entrance to Heaven. It was incredibly reassuring as well.

Another time, not too much later, I saw mom again. This time she saw me as well. She was up on some sort of mezzanine, a gorgeous marble balcony like you might see in a beautiful palace.

She was looking down at me and waving. Then she said something to me before she waved goodbye. She said, "They're going to let me look in on you from time to time."

Yet we didn't converse. I was thinking it was because I was still down on earth looking up at her on that beautiful terrace. Therefore, I'm guessing we couldn't have a conversation with each other because of that.

I just had time to wave back before she walked away and disappeared from the balcony.

I felt such peace and joy as I could clearly see in every way how great she felt! Relief for her flooded over me.

Kat Kerr is another person you can view on YouTube, who has gone to heaven also. Believe it or not, she describes a similar place that she refers to as, "the portal".

Kat describes the portal as a place where Heavenly citizens can go to look down on family and friends still back here on earth. Which is exactly what my mom was doing when I saw her.

What seemed to be the portal my mother was looking down through was very large and very spacious. That was the case with each level. For my mother was on the second level mezzanine or balcony. This wide-open space was obviously needed for many people to gather. I often saw great crowds of people and angels come together collectively to cheer on those, as I had mentioned before, who were serving the Lord, or had accepted Him as their Lord and Saviour! I've also seen masses of Heavenly citizens look down through such a portal at people on earth that they are waiting on to arrive in Heaven.

So rest assured earthlings! People you know that have passed on are still caring about you and watching out for you.

The main thing, and the most important for me to find out, was I got to see that my mom had made it to Heaven and that she was happy and doing just fine. My mom definitely deserved this eternal vacation.

She had a long and fulfilled life full of, yes, hardships but also pleasures. I'm glad she's finally getting to enjoy eternity in Heaven!

Wedges

Another time in Heaven, I was with a whole bunch of angels singing and praising. We were on some sort of massive balcony with pillars reaching up into the mist. You could look over the ledge down to earth below. It was similar to the one my mother had stood on when she looked down at me on earth.

I was sharing with Jesus how I'd noticed people on earth that I knew of were becoming overly irritable with each other. Sisters were arguing between each other. Mothers and daughters were arguing, fathers and sons arguing. Bosses with employees, employees amongst employees. And so on and so forth with everybody constantly and senselessly bickering. It was quite noticeable to me and I both sensed and felt it.

As we discussed this the Lord said, "Well then, go over to the ledge and start pulling out wedges between the people that you see down below on earth."

Sure enough, as I looked down over them, wedges were quite visible in between people. So, I began doing just that. It was easy to see where I should start pulling wedges out!

Not surprisingly when I returned to earth, I began noticing changes in the people that had been arguing previously. They were getting along! Wow, hallelujah!

Often my trips to Heaven were like that. (Where I had some kind of assigned job at hand to do.)

Other people that have been to Heaven seem to have grand tours. There were only a few times that kind of thing happened to me. I don't think I may have seen as much of Heaven as others have. Most of my time has been spent in the Throne Room or on walks with Jesus. At least so far.

When I need understanding, it will be imparted into my thoughts automatically. Up in Heaven, everyone is acting and operating in the will of God. On earth that is more of a rare thing.

My mission trip to Nepal a few years ago was a perfect example of a "Heavenly, lean, keen, Holy Spirit-filled team" of six of us. Each one of us was so tuned in to the Holy Spirit that we knew exactly what each of us was called to do. Each of us had gifts that were beautifully compatible.

We worked so well together that you could just sense the Holy Spirit moving throughout the whole crusade! In times like that, it's a real joy to work for the Lord, side-by-side with others that are doing the same. That is the ideal way Christians should interact with each other. I live for times like that!

A Blast for Our Senses

Sounds and Songs

In Heaven, the chirping birds and singing angels are exalted, far greater than all the choirs of earth put together. They all seem to respond for the pure joy of it! The sounds from the birds and angels are a glorious chanting! Such grand joy from these creatures has to come out! Such a beautiful sound! Have you ever been so excited you could just shout for joy? Well that's the kind of joy that abounds in Heaven. There's a worship song that I like to sing and when I sing it, I literally shout it out! The song goes something like this: "Shout to the Lord all the earth..."

The plants too, seem alive with the sheer joy of interacting with me. They seem to just bust out with such enthusiasm that it simply can't be contained. I get somewhat close to that kind of feeling when I'm out in nature. I get exuberance that bubbles up inside of me. Whether I'm in the mountains, in a forest or by a waterfall, I can't help but feel an over-abundance of inspirational exuberance!

It's the same way I feel sometimes when I'm filled to over- flowing with the Holy Spirit and worshipping my Lord. I simply can't contain it, and even if I tried, I would just have to burst out anyway and proclaim my love for my Lord!

I get a tingly feeling inside of me whenever I hear such glorious choirs of angels singing or even here on earth when I join in and sing songs of praise to my Lord with them!

It's like I become electrified! In fact, I've always felt as if my human body was holding me back from being able to sing the ultimate full-out way they sing in Heaven! I look forward to the day when my body will no longer be in the way.

A River of Living Water

One time in Heaven an angel showed me a river of living water. The water was crystal clear but not the kind of water here on earth. This water was LIVING water. Happy, uplifting water that flows through a person and comes directly from the Throne. For Jesus is the Living Water and because of Him, we will thirst no more.

I remember other times being in what seemed to be the same river splashing around and feeling completely and spiritually uplifted in every possible way! Jesus told me Himself, I need not ever leave the river. That was a profound revelation to me and a gold nugget to live by. For best results when walking in your faith, stay in the river to be fueled and filled up by the "living water". Translated, this means remain in Him and thirst no more!

There were trees along both sides of the river. However, I'm not sure whether they were the "trees of life" as described in John Burke's book or not?[3] He had stated that they were on both sides of the river, and that meant that there was more than one tree of life.

The Landscape

Many others claim to have seen exactly what scripture says in, (Rev. 7:9, 17, 21:10 and 22:1-2) "...a beautiful place of mountains, streams, trees, and amazing grass."

One person, Marv Besteman, that loved to play golf, noticed the grass in particular. He said that you notice how perfect, how "verdant, luscious the grass is at the Master's (golf tournament) and then try to imagine grass far greener and more deluxe. That's how green the grass is in Heaven." [4]

John Burke, in his book even tells of how, "A colour-blind British NDE'er suddenly "saw beauty in all kinds of colours with a new vision..." [5]

Grass and Colours

The grass and the colours in Heaven are spectacular! It deserves this little bit of extra time just to describe it.

---

[3] Pg 114, Imagine Heaven by J. Burke.

[4] pg 114, Imagine Heaven by J. Burke

[5] pg 114, Imagine Heaven by J. Burke

When I'm in Heaven, it's like I step on the blades of grass, but I don't really. I don't actually step on them like we do here on earth. They don't seem to get touched in Heaven, and nothing goes brown or rots, nor does it die.

Not only is the grass amazing! Everything's amazing. Things I've never seen before! That's what makes this book hard to write. Just try describing something that's not here on earth to people here on earth and see how easy it is. It isn't! The things I saw in Heaven can't be compared to things on earth.

I can tell you the grass and the radiantly coloured flowers are incredible and beautiful. Yet, when I tell you that Heaven's grass is greener than you've ever seen, "fluorescently greener". I don't know if you're able to truly get the picture of what I'm trying to describe.

I guess I'll just have to leave it to your fantastic imagination to come up with a green that is beyond all the greens here on earth! I trust you can do that!

In Heaven the fruit on the trees doesn't ever grow old. It doesn't rot and fall off. If you pick an apple, it comes off nicely and is replaced immediately by another perfectly ripe and delicious apple. The fruit doesn't have to grow, it just appears ready to eat.

One tree provides a variety of apples! Not just one kind!

There are many other fruits there that I have never seen on earth before. One doesn't have to work or harvest the plants in order to obtain the fruits of their labour. For there is no labour!

I don't have to dig any produce out of the ground to obtain it either. I just have to reach out and it appears in my hand.

Like a carrot for example, I don't even have to wash the dirt off the carrot before I eat it. It's ready to eat!

Butterscotch in Heaven

On one occasion in Heaven, shortly after my bunny, Butterscotch had died, I saw her! My heart fluttered with joy at what I saw!

It was a beautiful, lush green meadow full of many colourful and bright fragrant flowers. There were a whole bunch of different bunnies hopping around. Some nibbling on the grass here and there and everywhere. Some more solid colours of black and brown and white and grey. Others were spotted black and white or brown and white. Others even calico coloured with black, white, gold, and brown spots all over them. Some were really fluffy and furry, with long floppy rabbit ears, while others had shorter ears.

Butterscotch herself was frolicking all around the meadow. Hippin' and hoppin' and kicking up her heels, as she flicked her tail. Leaping in the air as she always did when she was happy go lucky. It delighted me greatly to see her so happy and carefree!

Colours

The green of the plants in Heaven is the greenest of greens I've ever seen. The intensity of this colour implies the plants are more than alive. Not the usual kind of alive grass and flowers here on earth. Rather they seem to take on a greater life. One in which they respond to my presence and also know what I'm thinking. It's as if they know I'm admiring each and every one of them.

I'm the kind of person that loves to stop and smell the roses. I will go into a flower shop that I pass by just to smell the roses. So, when I'm around the plants in Heaven, I admire every single one of them separately.

As I encounter meadows that stretch on in front of me seemingly endlessly, I observe that there's not only every flower that's on earth, but other ones with colours I wasn't aware of before visiting Heaven.

I was very preoccupied with checking every single one of them out as Jesus and I strolled through the garden on a path of gold during one of our walks.

Another NDE'er shared their description of the colours they saw: "I saw colours I had never seen before. The light wasn't the kind that he had ever seen before. It differs from any other kind, such as sunlight. It was white and extremely bright, and yet you could easily look at it. It's the pinnacle of everything there is. Of energy, of love especially, of warmth, as beauty. I was immersed in a feeling of total love. From the moment the light spoke to me, I felt really good, secure, and loved.

The love which came from it is just unimaginable, indescribable." [6]

This correlates with what I saw, and with what others have seen. A paradise that I felt in its awesome grandeur!

I too experienced all of the previous descriptions of the light and the colours and music. Only I did not go through any tunnel to get there like many NDE'ers tell their readers. There is beautiful music, colours unseen here on earth and that warm shiny energizing light unlike any other.

One way I might best describe these unusual colours to you would be to say some of them look like those bright colours that you can make from using fluorescent gel pens. Other colours look more like the metallic iridescent, shiny coloured gel pens.

I've tried to do justice by illustrating with words in this book, some of the grandeur I am so desperately trying to articulate with the limited English language I have. The English language does not have sufficient words to describe the magnificent things one sees in Heaven.

Captain Dale Black says it best: "if millions of jewels had been gathered into one place and the brightest sunlight shone through them, it wouldn't begin to describe the colours I saw.

[6] pg. 149, Imagine Heaven by J. Burke.

Heaven was filled with a rainbow of hues and provided me with a sensory feast." [7]

I would have to say it is a sensory and optical feast for sure!

As I earlier stated my editor Coralie Banks suggested that I write this book using many illustrations. Even if there were pictures, it would be hard to depict accurately. The colours we have on earth, no matter how beautiful, are limited compared to the ones in Heaven.

Take the green of the grass I described earlier. Heaven's "green", is so much greener, brighter, and actually alive! Heaven's green has an energy to it. It has a light that intensifies in brightness and that sparkles. It emanates continual freshness. It's as if each blade of grass is a jewel sparkling in the sunlight.

I've always admired plants on earth in a way that I hope they will get some vibe from me that tells them (as I do for animals as well) I'm grateful for them. I often whisper a grateful prayer of thankfulness for them for their bountiful beauty.

The flowers in Heaven seem to come alive with JOY as I admire them. It's as if they get their joy from me enjoying them and not just from God alone. This is profound to me, to say the least.

---

[7] pg. 105, Flight to Heaven by Captain D. Black.

Along with the enthusiasm coming from the plants is a movement that signifies not just life, but an intense energy. An energy that I interpret as joy. As astounding as this may sound, they even seem to hum, especially when all of Heaven breaks into song, which I discovered happens often.

The fragrances are mind-blowingly exotic! A perfume beyond perfumes.

I've always felt that if I had money to burn on earth, I would have a bouquet of flowers sent to my place every two weeks or so. However, if I were to pick a Heavenly bouquet it would last forever and never die.

There's no death in Heaven! There aren't any aging spots or blemishes on the flora and fauna. No bent or broken leaf, flower, or branch. Each plant is perfect.

And that's not all. When I walk through the meadows, the plants and grass I step on don't flatten, and can't be harmed in any way.

Others have seen and written about this. In "Imagine Heaven", Burke, the author shares Richard's description which also describes much of what I saw. He, (Richard), even "...picked a flower and when he put it back down, it was immediately replanted and growing again." [8]

[8] pg. 117, Imagine Heaven by J. Burke.

I recall another book, where they had a similar experience to mine. That person described their experience when picking some fruit off a tree in Heaven. The tree produced another one right behind it in the very same place. Wow! How deliciously cool is that?

"The fruit was pear shaped and copper coloured... When I touched the front to my lips, it evaporated and melted into the most delicious thing I had ever tasted." [9]

The author goes on to depict a beautifully manicured park filled with huge, striking trees. They had to be at least two thousand feet tall. And there were many different varieties.

Even Dr. Richard Eby who considered himself an amateur botanist, couldn't name all of the varieties of trees and flowers he saw during his NDE. He also noticed a new type of life in the flora. [10]

I too, have seen many varieties. I'm familiar with some, but I've no idea what species others are.

I like this about Heaven, and he shared this also. "There was a continual sound of chimes coming from the leaves of one type of tree as they brushed against one another." [11]

---

[9] pg. 117, Imagine Heaven by J. Burke - #12, Chapter 8.
[10] pg. 116, Imagine Heaven by J. Burke - #11, Chapter 8.
[11] pg. 117, Imagine Heaven by J. Burke - #12, Chapter 8.

There's a verse in the Bible that states something to the fact that if we don't praise and celebrate God. The leaves of the trees, plants, and the very earth will sing and shout for joy in celebration. (Isaiah 44:23)

Why do I love this part? Well, not just because others saw or heard this too, but mainly for the fact that all of the objects in Heaven, whether they have a heartbeat or not, chime in and celebrate in song or rhythm or humming of some kind as a form of praise and worship throughout Heaven.

That means all of Heaven is in worship, praise, and song in honour of God at any given moment anywhere and everywhere!

I really don't know whether they have a heartbeat or not. They could very well have a heartbeat because even the objects seem to be alive. Everything is alive in Heaven!

According to one of the stories from NDE'ers that I read, Richard, a messianic Jew, saw the flowers he stepped on stand right up inside his own feet and legs! They simply passed through one another. [12]

Maybe it's because I have not had a NDE like so many others, that I haven't personally seen the grass pass through my feet. Yet I did see that the blades of grass did not seem to get trampled at all. By the way, it smells like fresh cut grass all the time.

[12] pg. 116, Imagine Heaven by J. Burke - #11, Chapter 8.

You know how in the springtime the grass turns green again, and seems to be so much greener than ever, and so fresh and new? That's what the green land in Heaven looks like all the time! It never loses that freshness. It never gets dusty or old looking.

No part of Heaven needs the sun or the moon to shine on it to provide light by day or night. There is no day or night needed. The glory of God is sufficient and so bright He needs to dim it for me.

My Hovering Difference

"A brilliant light appeared in the room and a serene peace came over me... I had the feeling of being drawn up and leaving my body and I looked back and I saw it lying there on the bed while I was going up towards the ceiling of the room." [13]

The NDE'ers that I read about experienced hovering in one way, but mine was completely different.

I had an experience, whereby I was taken up and hovered over my bed. Only when I looked back at the bed, I was not there! So, I experienced the same thing as other NDE'ers have, however they saw their human body on the bed or operating table, whereas I did not see myself in the bed at all. There was nothing there, the bed was empty.

[13] pg. 154, Imagine Heaven by J. Burke.

I concluded that what I had undergone was different because I hadn't died, whereas others had literally flat-lined and died and were no longer in their physical body.

Before the hovering experience, I'd been terribly ill in bed, and I was praying fervently to the Lord to either take me home or make me better.

After my experience hovering, I asked the Lord if hovering with no body left behind was like the Rapture. He did not answer me but just smiled mysteriously with an all-knowing look.

That Brilliant Light

Vicky: was blind but she was able to see when in Heaven. She saw how grand and magnificent He was. She also stated that she had "a non-physical body... made of light." [14]

That is something that did not happen to me. I think it didn't because I hadn't had an NDE.

Nor did I go through a tunnel to a light as others may have, for, I think, the very same reason. I hadn't physically died. Since compiling this book, I have come across others similar to me in that they did not die either. Very interesting, and good to learn.

I just went from earth to someplace in Heaven just like that. There was this incredible light! Definitely something that was

[14] pg. 33, Imagine Heaven by J. Burke.

tangible as well as extremely opalescent and visible! I could feel its energy along with peacefulness. It fed and nourished me, not only physically but mentally and emotionally.

Since the light emanated from God, it was also full of love and peace and had a safeness about it. This light didn't just shed light on everything, it provided an awareness about everything. The light filled me with love at the same time as it gave me a perfect peace and "okayness".

People and Appearances

"Airline captain Dale Black noticed that he saw them, (Heavenly people) for who they really were. None were skinny, none overweight. None were crippled, none were bent or broken. None were old, none were young. If I had to guess I would say that they appear to be somewhere around 30 years old... Although some form of time does seem to exist in Heaven, no one aged." [15]

I saw all races of people during the different times I visited Heaven. Heaven was multicultural in every way!

Much the same was described on page 114 of John Burke's book. "... People from every nation and tribe and people and language... clothed in white robes and held palm branches in their hands." [16]

Something university professor Howard Storm, described during his NDE may give insight into the appearance of age in

[15] pg. 94, Imagine Heaven by J. Burke.
[16] pg. 114, Imagine Heaven by J. Burke.

Heaven. Brilliant beings of light he called "the saints and angels" came to meet him and said, "We can appear to you in our human form if you wish or in any form you want, so you will be comfortable with us."

Storm answered, "No. Please... You're more beautiful than anything I've ever seen." [17]

This confirms for me the theory I have, that they will appear in a way that is most comfortable for us as individuals. Jesus will appear to you in a way that you're most comfortable with. Hence, as I said earlier, I am reluctant to describe Jesus to other people for that reason. Each is apt to see Him in an entirely different way that will be comfortable for them.

If any of you readers have read the book, "The Shack", by Wm. Paul Young, he describes his Trinity in what is considered a controversial way. God appears as a black matriarch! "A large beaming African American woman." Then... " a small distinctively Asian woman appeared... A third person emerges, he appeared Middle Eastern and was dressed like a labourer complete with tool belt and gloves"! [18]

However, I myself was not shocked or taken aback by it at all! It did not matter to me that God appeared to him as an African American woman nor that the Holy Spirit appear as an Asian woman and Jesus himself as a Middle Eastern carpenter.

[17] pg. 94, Imagine Heaven by J. Burke.
[18] pg. 84 & 86, The Shack by Paul Young.

For I believe the Trinity will appear to you, a unique individual, in the way you'll be comfortable with.

Made In His Image

We humans are in fact eternal creatures like the angels. Yet unlike the angels, we are being given many, many trials in our path to choose life instead of death eternally. (Deuteronomy 30:19-20)

Many could ask, why would a loving God allow so much evil, pain and suffering on this earth? Because it's meant to be a warning for us and a chance to choose Him! And frankly it's my opinion that we wouldn't know what good is without knowing and experiencing bad.

There's something much worse. When we choose to follow ourselves, and reject Him as God, then we're on our own! For He doesn't want to take away the freedom of choice He's given us.

That makes sense to me because I can see He would want us to choose Him of our own free will.

I read somewhere that God did not create hell for humans. He created hell for the fallen one-third of the eternal angels who made a choice to rule themselves. So, hell is where they rule.

Currently, the Holy Spirit can help us keep our evil inclinations in check on earth through our conscience. "He will guide you into all truth." (John 16:8; 16:13)

What Clothes Will I Wear?

Everyone that I saw in Heaven was wearing robes of some sort. Therefore, I suspect that's the type of clothes I will wear in Heaven. The white of the robes seemed to be glowing and alive! They would wave or sway in a rhythm of praise and worship with an energy of love if that makes sense.

Jesus said in the book of Revelation, "...they will walk with me, dressed in white, for they are worthy. The one who is victorious will, like them, be dressed in white clothing; and I will never blot out the name of that person from the book of life, but will acknowledge that name before my Father and his angels." (Revelation 3:4-5).

John the apostle said of his experience of Heaven, "there before me was a great multitude that no one could count, from every nation, tribe, people and language, standing before the throne and before the lamb Jesus. They were wearing white robes and were holding palm branches in their hands... (Revelation 7:9)

More Similarities

When I go to Heaven I don't die (albeit temporarily) like many others that have had NDE's report. Yet, there's something about me that changes, just like them. I seem to feel and to be perfect both inside and out! I feel super healthy. I seem to have super, holy, intelligence and insight and awareness!

It's like I can see everything around me and be aware of it without actually seeing it. There's no hurt, no pain, no negative thinking whatsoever crosses my mind, nor does it seem to exist around me in any way, shape, or form.

All of this I feel in Heaven and some of it I retain here on earth.

The people in Heaven appear not to be solid. They seem to be in their bodies like I would see them on earth, but they aren't in the flesh. I don't know if it is a hologram sort of state, I'm not sure what that is.

I've noticed that they eat things and enjoy them or smell them. They seem to have all their senses, but it is like they didn't really need to eat, it's just for enjoyment. Everything is for enjoyment; it is just awe inspiring. What a paradise! A Paradise above and beyond my dreams.

There isn't a need to do anything. No jobs to get up and go to work at. There's just a desire to rest in enjoyment. I guess I would have to say Heaven is the most stress-free place in the universe!

I have gratitude that flows through me that's reciprocated to me through everything. I have need for nothing.

Most of the time, I'm specifically there in Heaven to enjoy and soak up some R&R, as a break from the stress down on earth. Not that I don't have stress-free time on earth sometimes, or ways to take a break and rest from the stress. It's an additional bonus to receive it in Heaven as well.

Walking With Jesus

One of the things I enjoyed the most on my trips to Heaven was walking with Jesus. Sometimes we walked in the beautiful meadows. Other times in another beautiful part of Heaven. Sometimes, maybe along a walkway in flowery gardens. The surroundings varied, but it was all extremely exquisite and perfectly manicured like nothing I've ever seen before.

I never thought of this before. I had just assumed that these parks and gardens just existed in Heaven. And they do, however, Jesus Christ brought this thought to my attention. Jesus Christ reminded me that when I went with Him to Heaven on these walks the gardens just appeared AROUND us! I had not thought of it that way before. Yet it makes sense because we don't have to work or make any efforts at all in Heaven. Hence if we want to go for a walk in a park, it is effortless! We don't have to GO THERE. We just have to think it and voila! The park or garden we want to walk in appears before us!

Other times together Jesus and I would simply lay right in the clouds!

You know how children lie on the grass and look up into the clouds and ponder life at times? Well, Jesus and I would just lay in the clouds and look up into Heaven and talk and talk and talk, without a word said.

Those are times I learned so much about my spirituality and how much more I can still learn.

I needn't be anxious or ask a bunch of questions all of a sudden because I know they are going to be answered automatically. Hence there was no anxiety of any kind. No concerns of any kind. Problems evaporated!

When Jesus takes me to these places He often comforts and embraces me. It is with so much warmth and love. "I am convinced that nothing can ever separate us from God's love. Neither death nor life, neither angels nor principalities of demons, neither our fears for today nor our worries about tomorrow. Nor height, nor depth, nor any other created thing, will be able to separate us from God which is Christ Jesus our Lord. Not even the powers of hell can separate us from God's love." (Romans 8:38-39)

His eyes are such loving warm eyes. It is like they permeate every part of me, empathizing with me in every way. By the way, I was incapable of lying about anything. Yet I want to reveal everything to Him.

He knows everything about me and knows all about the so-called skeletons in my closet. Whether I tell Him or not, it wouldn't matter. He still knows!

What I like about it is, I don't have to hide anything from Him!

I wasn't spared judgement, however. Surprisingly, it was a relief to deal with it and get it out-of-the-way once and for all. We went back through my life and he showed me places where I had been unfair or cruel to others. Or jealous and/or envious. I recall feeling deep regret and falling on my knees to ask for forgiveness, not only from Jesus but if I could, from those I had harmed.

"Even though I walk through the valley of the shadow of death, I should fear no evil. For you are with me; your rod and your staff, they comfort me." (Psalm 23:4)

"My God, in whom I trust and on whom I rely…" (Psalm 91:2).

I love that He knows everything! It is so freeing. I cannot tell everybody everything for I know better than to cast my thoughts anywhere. Yet, I can tell Him and discuss such private things freely with Him.

We often communicate without words and we often share thoughts just with a glance.

I feel safe beyond measure with Him!

"Be still and know that I am God." (Psalm 46:10)

Jesus Steering Me

This one was a rather unusual walk if I must say so myself. Jesus decided this particular time to take me through a review of my life, going all the way back to when I was about three or four years old and living on a ranch.

I had asked Jesus at other times to show me how He's protected me and gone before me. This particular walk was to show me how He had guided me through my life all these years, without me even realizing it! (Here's another gold nugget for you. God is watching over you right now, whether you know Him or not!)

Jesus knew me way back on the ranch before I even knew He existed! How do I know? He showed me!

Sometime shortly after my divorce in my early 40s, Jesus took me through a slideshow of my life from about 1995, all the way back to when I was about three or four years old playing on the ranch in the barn loft.

One specific time, the slide show depicted the year I moved into the students' residence at the University of Alberta for the first year of my B. Ed degree.

I recall penciling in to go to church one of the first Sundays after moving into the residence. I headed out one Sunday morning in one direction. My plan was to attend the very first church I came to. If I didn't like that church, then I would simply go to the next one the following Sunday until I found one that I liked.

What Jesus showed me in the mini slideshow of my life was me walking along the street just outside the university residence. As I walked, I came up to a large building that looked sort of like a church. As I pondered upon it, the slideshow showed me exactly what had actually happened.

It showed Jesus putting His hands on both of my shoulders and steering me clear of that church. As it turned out, that church was one I should steer clear of (pun intended! LOL!)

The slideshow indicated very clearly that Jesus steered me clear of going into that building. I found out years later it was not a Christian church and definitely not one that I should attend.

There were a number of these types of incidents that occurred in the slideshow. It was comforting to know that Jesus had kept a close eye on my progression all this time. He very subtly and lovingly would steer me in the right direction as I went through the events of my life. This was something I took great joy and comfort in knowing. That He was looking out for me so carefully without me even being aware of it at the time.

The slideshow concluded with the most beautiful ending I could possibly have discovered about my life and my childhood. It was the last image Jesus showed me in the mini slideshow of my life.

He took me back to the ranch. I was about four years old, in the loft of our barn on our ranch. Here is where I often played with my imaginary friend. In the slideshow, Jesus had me in the loft standing there beside Him. He pointed across the loft in the opposite direction from where we were standing.

There standing and smiling at me, was my imaginary playmate who I had all those years ago. You are not going to believe who it was? It was Jesus himself! Oh my Lord God in Heaven! I actually had Jesus for my imaginary friend all those years ago when I was a young child on the ranch. Wow!

What joy, peace, and comfort I received from this privilege to watch a mini slideshow review of my life! How wonderful that He was there every moment, watching over me and keeping me safe.

God knows everything! "Oh Lord, you have searched me and know me. You know when I sit down and when I rise up, you understand my thoughts from afar, you scrutinize my path and my lying down and you are intimately acquainted with all my ways, even before there is a word on my tongue behold, the Lord you know it all." (Psalm 139:1-4)

The Rickety Bridge

Now I am not exactly sure this next story actually took place in Heaven. Yet I am pretty sure. There are only two reasons I am unsure. One, the bridge was old, rickety, and appeared ready to fall apart when someone so much as stepped on it. Nothing else in Heaven is old and broken down! Not a thing!

The other reason was I went to run back to tell others, which made me think I was on earth when this happened.

However, it just dawned on me that Jesus can make anything happen and set the stage for anything to occur in Heaven in order to illustrate something to me. It was one of the most incredible and very important lessons He could've taught me.

It all began while we were taking one of our walks in Heaven along a nice path in the mountains. We weren't in a garden this time at all, contrary to where we usually took our strolls.

Jesus did something different than He usually does. He removed His arm from around my shoulders and walked on ahead of me and disappeared around the corner.

He had never gone ahead like that before!

For a nano-second I thought it odd, but I was certainly not concerned. I never question what my Lord does. I've learned over the years to trust without question because I have enough evidence to know for sure that He knows best!

By the time I got around the corner, He had already made it across a long skinny rope bridge. He was standing just off from the bridge way on the other side. When He saw me, He beckoned for me to follow Him across the bridge.

Now you need to know I personally am not really fond of these swinging narrow wood and rope bridges that cross great crevices in canyons. So, you'd think I would hesitate at the foot of the bridge and resist following Him across the rest of the way. Especially given the condition of the broken down rotten, rickety, bridge!

But I didn't hesitate one bit! I charged right across and over to Him. I was completely confident, knowing that if He went across the bridge and was beckoning me to come and follow Him, it was completely safe to do so and not to worry in the least about the bridge and how rickety and old and decrepit it looked.

Once across, I ran to Jesus. He was just beaming as He gave me a big, huge hug! The smile on His face indicated how pleased He was that I crossed so confidently across the bridge and up to Him just like that. He relayed to me how pleased He was by saying "well done my good and faithful!"

In that moment I had an instantaneous, good idea. I ran back across that bridge, again without hesitation. I just had to tell others to not be afraid. That it looks scary but is not and they will be OKAY! Just follow Him!

Things such as trials and troubles in life can look scary and unstable, but if Christ is leading the way you can trust completely in Him and be assured that it's all OK.

I've always equated it to being like a blind person on Jesus Christ's arm. A blind person relies on their guide to show them the way, not questioning whether they are being taken along a safe route or not.

Each time I made a trip to Heaven, it seemed like He knew I was ready for it. Each time I sensed I was going through trials and learning that would lead me to further experiences in Heaven. Jesus, knowing I was ready for another trip to Heaven, seemed particularly excited and delighted to be able to take me and show me around.

Innocence Restored

One time while I was in the Throne Room talking with God, He told me He created the earth for all mankind. He continued to say He created all of the earth for me to enjoy.

I laughed like that little innocent, gleeful, child I always am when I'm with Him in the Throne Room. Then He said with a smirk, "I made it all by myself too, LOL!" Then we both roared with laughter together!

He makes me feel so at ease when I'm with Him. I'm this innocent sin-free little child that can be just myself without having any critical condemnation come upon me whatsoever. Daddy/God, is so unconditional and so fun-loving to be with. I love these visits with him. When I leave the Throne Room, I leave so refreshed and renewed and ready to tackle the world out there, free of negativity.

Each time I've made a trip to Heaven, it seemed like He knew I was ready for it. Yet I myself didn't necessarily think this way.

Yet I know very well every time I come back from Heaven, I've definitely grown all the wiser from the experience. I realize that my visits to Heaven often connect to learning trials I'm going through here on earth.

Jesus, knowing I'm ready for another trip to Heaven, seems particularly excited to be able to take me and show me something new.

I sense that my most recent trip to Heaven is not the end of my visits, and that there's far more that He will delight in showing me when I'm ready.

The Banquet Table

On another trip to Heaven, Jesus took me to a banquet table. It was elaborate, luxurious, and massive. A grandiose banquet table that spanned off into the horizon as far as I could see. Oh my, how am I going to describe such a magnificent sight?

Picture a banquet table set for a queen or king. That would give you a very meagre description of the banquet table I was seated at. Take what that would look like to you, and multiply it by 100 times, and you might come close to the picture of what the table looked like.

The candelabras sparkled and gleamed in the surrounding warm loving white light as they strung out all the way down the center of the table as far as I could see. Each was adorned with seven lit elegantly engraved pearl candles. The plates and silverware were of the purest gold with silver embossed trim.

As I picked up the napkin on the plate in front of me, I could see it was engraved with silver and gold threads of beautiful tapestry. Each was placed decoratively at each place setting.

They spanned along all the way down as far as I could see. Between the candelabras, along the center of the table were small bunches of bright, colourful, fragrant, fresh flowers, bursting with aroma.

The wine goblets were of a rich filigreed gold. Beside them were glistening, singing crystal water glasses. Yes, they actually seem to sing. I could hear a nice, pleasant soft humming coming from each of them in unison.

The tablecloth was of an opulent red velvet embroidered with a golden fringe. Each chair was upholstered with rich matching red velvet. The cushion and backing were framed with a lovely golden lush wood, engraved with stunning fruits and flowers cascading down along the legs and along the arms as well as the back that stretched up like a crown over my head.

Jesus escorted me arm-in-arm up to the head of the table and sat me down in the head chair. He was a real gentleman, pulling the chair out and letting me sit down and then pushing me and the chair up to the table.

As I sat in the head chair, a glamorous deep rich velvet, royal purple robe appeared on me. It reminded me of the kind of robe a king would wear.

Then Jesus placed a regal crown on my head. The crown reminded me of what a king would be crowned with. It had exquisite, sparkling gems of every colour surrounded by gleaming rich gold.

All the gems and gold glistened and shone, sparkling in the beautiful white light that surrounded us as He placed the crown gently and lovingly on my head.

Somehow with words not even spoken, it seemed appropriate to have communion in gratefulness. Communion with Jesus, or rather the Trinity, is very moving for me!

He served me the wine in a beautiful Golden goblet. In my other hand is bread to represent his body, sacrificed for me! Sacrificed for all of us!

His Pierced Wounds

Speaking of jewels! This might be a good time to introduce the wonderful and fabulous story that Jesus shared with me about the pierced wounds in his hands and feet.

Much of the crucifixion would often sadden me. But over time when I realized that it was their plan all along, it wasn't so sad to me after all. In fact, I saw it as the Trinity's absolutely brilliant plan and victory!

Then when Jesus shared how proud He was of those once crusted over, dirt-filled holes and bloody pierced wounds, I took on a whole new joyful perspective of the crucifixion! For it is finished and was the Trinity's victory! Not satan's!

In fact, I've profoundly observed many a time when there have been tragic occurrences in the world. Then God seems to outsmart those tragedies and bring victory as a result!

In his righteous grand proudness, Jesus humbly spoke of His wounds. Then he placed His hands open on my lap.

I could see for myself how they had changed from dried, bloody wounds piercing through between the bones in His wrists. They were so beautiful instead!

From out of the bloody pierced wounds came beautiful gems cascading down from each hole. Rubies and emeralds embedded in filigreed gold! First were huge teardrop-like rubies coming out of the hole. They were surrounded by smaller teardrop and heart shaped gems of various sizes. All were set in beautiful gold tapestry! Absolutely exquisite, rubies, emeralds, and sapphires. You name it!

I was in complete awe and began to admire, of all things, those pierced wounds. Before, they used to sadden and disgust me. Now more than ever, I honour what He did for us. The sacrifice He made so that I would be free from death and sin, once and for all!

That is definitely something we ourselves could not possibly do on our own. Wow, what an ingenious, superb plan! No wonder Jesus is proud.

"With man, this is impossible, but not with God. All things are possible with God." (Mark 10:27)

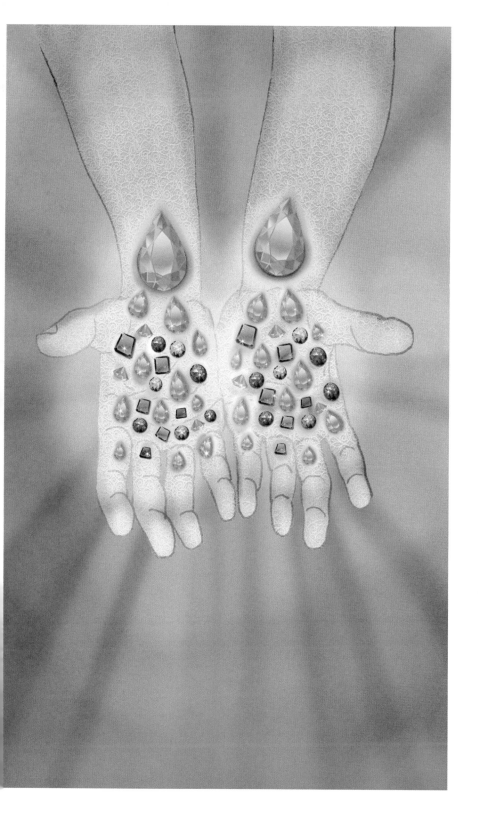

Connectedness

You can talk to Jesus and hear from Him; really and truly! I have been saying this almost since the time when I became a Christian at age 12, many years ago.

During our conversations He's said, "It is My desire and actually, your deepest need as human beings, to learn to live intimately with Me and the Trinity."

Hence, one of the things Jesus told me to do was to show other Christians how to do just that. To encourage them to become intimate with Him, Jesus Christ! Just as Adam and Eve walked with God in the garden of Eden.

He has also said during our times together, and I believe Him, "for this you and I were made." Therefore, this close relationship we must recover and accomplish within each of ourselves as Christians. It is innate within us as human beings to seek God. He created us in His image to be intimate because God wants us to talk to Him. Regularly, every day and because He loves us so much!

You may have heard the old saying: "Give someone a fish and you feed him for the day. Teach someone to fish and you feed him for the rest of his life."

The same holds true of life itself. If you give someone an answer, you help them solve one problem. But if you teach him to walk with God, then you've helped him solve the rest of his life. You've helped him to tap into an inexhaustible source of guidance, comfort, and protection. We can't possibly master enough principles and disciplines to ensure that life works out. We weren't meant to. We were meant to rely on our Trinity Father God.

That whole approach to life of trying to figure it out on our own, beat the odds, and get on top of our game is utterly godless. Definitely it is not walking with God in the garden in the cool of the day.

I'd just like to say here that it's great that I've been to Heaven a number of times and that others have too. Yet it really isn't something everybody needs to do to become intimate with Christ and the Trinity.

Whatever your situation, if you have the opportunity to develop a conversation and intimacy with the wisest, kindest, most generous not to mention perfect person in the world, wouldn't it make sense to spend your time with that person, as opposed to, say, slugging your way through life on your own?

He wants your love and trust, freely given. Your intimacy. And it's actually as simple as talking to Him.

That's the most fundamental basic form of prayer. And everybody knows how to pray that way!

I encourage you to wait no longer and pray by just plain talking to Him every day as if He's an imaginary friend but totally real. Let me assure you, He is totally real!

I've read many self-help Christian books. But overall, they just brought me right back to the same old conclusion that I always had right from when I was a child. And that is to simply get more and more intimate with my God the Father, Jesus Christ, and the Holy Spirit.

As I get older, I become more conscious of my liaison to Christ, my Father God, and the Holy Spirit. This is the intimacy I'm talking about. We need to personalize all three of them, the Trinity.

Heavenly Communication

We speak without speaking! Actually, it's like our thoughts are transmitted between each other. I don't have to state my questions to the angels that show me around or the people that I speak to. They just know. Nothing is hidden nor needs to be hidden.

Relax though! You don't need to worry about them hearing any of your thoughts good or bad, secretive or not. Not in any way because you just wouldn't have any negative thoughts in Heaven, I'm guessing, because I don't.

Heaven seems to erase all negativity and worrying thoughts. I have absolutely no concerns while there. Negativity just doesn't exist. It's a beautiful state of mind. A beautiful place to be in! And I don't just mean location, but state of mind as well.

We will be able to talk and sing like never before in Heaven! The most preferred way of communicating with God, angels, and people will be directly: heart to heart.

God tells the prophet Isaiah about Heaven's communication, saying, "Before they call, I will answer; while they are still speaking, I will hear" (Isaiah 65:24). Believe it or not, trust me, you can obtain this right here on earth! This actually does happen to me here on earth without having to go to Heaven.

People describe this in different ways, but it's uncanny how consistently NDE'ers described a nonverbal, perfect communication in Heaven.

It seems they don't have to be smart and they certainly aren't stupid. There was no such thing as dumb. No such thing as failure. It is like all the negatives that we encounter on earth can't arrive in Heaven and have to be shed as people enter in. There is only perfection for each of us to enjoy!

A Recent Trip

I had a very recent visit to Heaven. You'll recall God had said to me on my very first visit to Him, when Jesus had taken me by the hand that time, "You will come back and visit me won't you?"

It took me a while to get up enough nerve to go back and visit Him again. Now I have been to visit Him numerous times. It seems I often go to visit Him when I want comforting and healing. He's like my Daddy that I run to, to fix a boo-boo.

This recent time I went to see Him though, was a time I wanted to run and share some good news with Him! I'd been to a church service where the pastor had actually fallen under the Holy Spirit and was lying on the floor at the front of the church.

I was so excited about this that I had to run and tell my Daddy, Father God. Yes, this pastor was actually resting in the spirit at the front of the church during a Sunday service! This really was unusual, and I'd never seen it before. To me it was an indication that the pastor was willing to step outside of his religious box. To become more like what our Father God hopes for us.

He hopes for us to have freedom in our faith to follow the promptings of the Holy Spirit, regardless of whether they are uncomfortable to do or see.

I just had to run and tell Him all about it. I was encouraged by this. Of course, the pastor wasn't leading the service that Sunday. There was a guest speaker up at the pulpit. The pastor was not standing at the pulpit at the time that he fell under the Spirit. However, I'm always excited and pleased with the progress in any pastor's freedom from religion, and from a religious spirit. I was thrilled to be able to run to my Daddy God and tell him all about what I saw.

I knew He would be thrilled to hear this breakthrough news. After all, He prays for us to become free in our faith from religious do's and don'ts. Instead He desires for us to gain a personal connection to Him.

You may recall that I referred to a couple of times that Jesus gets concerned or sad for us. As the time grows closer to Him coming again, He needs us to tune more into Him and less into religion.

As God prays for us to personalize our relationship with Him, so do I pray it for others, and of course always for myself, to never drift from His side.

Finally, Freedom and Joy

I haven't seen all of Heaven, nor some of the things that others have seen. I suspect we'll have the opportunity in Heaven to see all of earth's projects, inventions, endeavours, discoveries and most of all God's hand in all of them! Who knows? Maybe there'll be 3-D movies showing on creation and other such amazing things.

I look forward to others joining me in thinking outside of the box, because we will have total freedom to do so in Heaven! I look forward to great long chats with people like Einstein, Tesla, and Mary Magdalene, etc. Nothing will hold us back. (By the way, I have to say here as a side note. Mary Magdalene was not a prostitute and she was older!)

Just as Jesus Christ said, "I have come that you will have life and life more abundantly!" (John 10:10) not only in Heaven but here on earth as well.

Finally. Life the way we were meant to relate to it and experience it, in all its perfection. We will finally see ourselves the way Jesus Christ and God, see us. Yeah! We get to be who we really are!

No more negativity, condemnation, or judgement in any form whatsoever. For none exists in Heaven! We will finally get to see and comprehend beyond our understanding here on earth. (Proverbs 3:5-6)

Heaven is filled with all that we could ever need. Everything is provided. Unimaginable things far, far greater, than we have on earth. Things that we can't even imagine exist, do exist!

The Core Near Death Experiences

I've included this confirming information because it provides great comparisons. All but number 1, 4, and 12 below were common elements of my experiences. I quoted most of the items from John Burke's book, "Imagine Heaven".

"Although no two experiences are like… there are amazingly common elements to the core near death experiences described…" (in all the books I have read.) "…by young or old, across cultures, in different languages." Even "…researchers and individuals … agree on the core experience."

Dr. Long reports on the percentage of each core element described in his study of 1300 NDE's from around the world:

1. Out of body experience: separation of consciousness from the physical body: 75.4%
2. Heightened senses. 74.4% said "more conscious and alert than normal."
3. Intense and generally positive emotions or feelings of incredible peace: 76.2%

4. Passing into or through a tunnel: 33.8%
5. Encountering a mystical or brilliant light: 64.6%
6. Encountering other beings, either mystical beings or deceased relatives or friends: 57.3%
7. A sense of alteration of time or space: 60.5%
8. Life review: 22.2%
9. Encountering otherworldly "Heavenly "realms": 52.2%
10. Encountering or learning special knowledge: 56%
11. Encountering a boundary or barrier: 31%
12. A return to the body. 58.5% were aware of the decision to return. [19]

---

[19] pg. 46, *Imagine Heaven* by J. Burke.

Logical Conclusion

"Anyone who doesn't believe in miracles is not a realist," [20] says David Ben-Gurion in the book, "To Heaven and Back", by Dr. Mary Neal.

Many question whether God is present and contemporary in our world today. I am convinced, given the miracles I have observed in my life, He certainly is! Plus the miracles I personally received in my own body and life, you can bet He's contemporary!

My story and others that I've shared here are meant to reinforce some facts about Heaven that I hope will spur you on to want to seek Him out for yourself. "For you will never walk in darkness if you walk with Him...the light of the world." (John 8:12)

In His word, He promised that all who seek him whole-heartedly will find relationship with him, because God created us to have relationship with Him.

---

[20] pg. 75, To Heaven and Back by Dr. Mary Neal.

There are something like 5467 promises in the Bible God assures each of us of as individuals!

We don't have to go to Heaven. We can and should enter into relationship by faith, right here on earth. It's easy! Simply stating that you want to and will, is all our Father God needs us to do. Asking Him to come into our life is simply all we have to do to follow Him. Just turning to Him in faith. As scripture says, "... walk by faith not by sight..." (2 Corinthians 4:18).

God can speak straight to our thoughts right now! We can learn how to listen spiritually and as we respond and trust, we grow to know God in a more personal way.

To know and seek a relationship with God is innate within each of us. There is no greater thing than to have a close relationship with God!

Once we find the truth, and therefore God, then we will have freedom! Freedom here on earth as it is in Heaven, says the Lord!

Not just me but others that went to Heaven, also say similar things to what I have felt with God personally. He is so glorious and He's all light and love! His correcting is done in love and not condemnation, punishment, or hate. Nor am I shunned by my God or His angels for asking questions. There is no hellfire and brimstone!

It is disappointing and sad that those of us that have experienced opportunities to go to Heaven are reluctant to talk about it. It's a shame, but that that's the way it is. It's unfortunate that we can't be more open about our experiences. Actually, such news should be shouted from the Church steeples! Why do we dismiss the stories?

Why should we, and why do we consider them meaningless, of all things? In some of the books I read there was the implication that such experiences were counter to our Christian faith!

I maintain the exact opposite opinion. These stories are crucial to our faith! After all, the main purpose of Christianity is to depict the love of Christ, the Holy Spirit and Father God. What better way to do it than describe actual experiences in Heaven, where that rings true through and through? Wouldn't we want to know that there is a Heaven and God is there, full of love? And He is waiting to greet us with love that is overflowing, unconditional, and not condemning?

John Price states in his book, we should celebrate these near deaths. It counts as a living testament of God's many, glorious promises.

I'd like to see our Christian family encourage these stories to spread as testimony to the love and glorious gift of eternal life that God has for us.

Who wouldn't want to embrace the loving, forgiving nature of God?

All the books I read expressed a common fact that this loving embrace that God portrayed to each of the NDE'ers. Their race, culture, or FAITH didn't matter!

It is important that others hear about the stories because they are life changing, not just to the one who experiences such trips to Heaven, but for ALL mankind as well!

I like how John Price puts it in his book "Revealing Heaven" (and I'm so sorry I can't find the exact page): "It saddens me that there are those who refuse to believe the validity and reality of these reports. They are held hostage by outdated and even harmful attitudes about much in this world and the next." Like him, I feel privileged that I have not only experienced these trips myself, but I've been greatly changed for the better! That is my I hope for you too!

My testimony and others that I've shared here are meant to reinforce that fact and to spur you on in a good way to want to seek Him out for yourself. "For you will never walk in darkness if you walk with Him, ...the light of the world." (John 8:12). In His word, He promised that all who seek Him wholeheartedly will find relationship with Him, because God created us to have relationship with Him.

To repeat: We don't have to go to Heaven. We can and should enter into this relationship by faith, right here on earth. It's easy! Simply stating you want to and will, is all our Father God requires for us to freely do.

God can speak straight to our thoughts right now! We can learn how to listen spiritually, and as we respond and trust, we grow to know God in a more personal way.

My prayer for you is that He, Jesus Christ, becomes so real for you that you won't need to go to Heaven like I did to experience that realness in your close relationship with Him. The more you get to know Him, the more you'll have the realness of Christ in your life.

That's what is most important, and what I pray for you to have.

Amen!

Aspirations

For whatever reason, the big guy in the sky thinks I should reveal these stories now. The time has finally arrived to go ahead and share with you these marvelous and incredible visits to Heaven, never before revealed!

What I unveil here may increase your hope, regardless of your race, culture, or faith. Your life after death can have a positive outcome!

My visits are meant to reinforce that fact and spur you on in a good way to want to checkout and seek God for yourself. God promises all who seek Him wholeheartedly, WILL find relationship with Him, because God created us to have that relationship. It's innate within us to seek Him.

Regardless of the choices you've made, or how afraid or ashamed you may feel deep down in the privacy of your being, He will welcome you with open arms and unconditional love.

That's the very best news!

Made in the USA
Coppell, TX
05 July 2022

79585427R00064